This Journal Belongs To:

Name ______________________________

Address ____________________________

____

Phone ______________________________

Email ______________________________

We hope you enjoyed using this book. It would really help us a lot if you would take a moment to leave a review. Thanks!

Snippy Chuckles Journals
Ha! Ha! Very Funny!
Ready for another chuckle?
Check out our book catalog at:

amazon.com/Snippy-Chuckles-Journals/e/B07PWQQZQX

Made in United States
Troutdale, OR
02/26/2024

18009765R00062